Longing for the Snow...

Poetry

ERIK VAN ACHTER

James Brian Moulder
-Drawings-

Immature poets imitate;
Mature poets steal.

T.S. ELIOT - The Sacred Wood

For all the people who work in *the John Hay Library* and in *the Brown University Bookstore.* Your workplace was my place of inspiration.

For all the people who work at the Portuguese Department. Working with you was a privilege.

Briosa!

Erik

Contents

Foreword.

Longing for the Snow is a poetic rendering of my stay at Brown University in the winter and fall of the year 2018. I had been there before, various times, as part of a chopped up postdoctoral stay at the Portuguese Department. Each time with a different Grant, each time in different house and each time in a different mood.
2018 was different in that I kept a "poetic" journal. I mean that I tried to write a poem – or something which looked like a poem- every night when I arrived home, based on the impressions I wrote down in my Brown Notebook during the day. (Mostly in the Hay Library or the Brown Bookstore over a Blue State coffee).
Re- reading the book written with a vintage parker fountain pen, is the result of mixed blessings: nostalgia and exhilaration, hope and despair, rage and sadness. Above all it is a recording of Menière's disease, first diagnosed around 2010 and which I have been suffering from ever since, but which must have been at its height in 2018. Most poems deal with the beautiful season of autumn on the East Coast of the U.S.A and with some of the buildings or monuments which impressed me or had a special meaning for me while I fought the disease or simply caught my imagination while I was daydreaming. *Longing for the Snow* is so to speak also a therapeutic journey beyond the nausea, the gradual lack of equilibrium and problems with sound perception.
Therapeutic too is one poem about a collegiate wrestler I met and with whom I had a good connection ignoring the fact he was a wrestler. He also appears in my short story "The Coney Island Ice-cream Eater" in the collection *Billy Rubin and Other Stories*. A

minor concussion with dire consequences killed him while staying alive. The dramatic circumstances have had an enormous impact on me and brought me to collegiate wrestling. It also brought me to medicine in an effort to understand what I had witnessed. I would love to thank William Allison whose tutorials were of great help. I should mention that the poem *snow globe* is the result of a Sunday afternoon conversation. Specials thanks to Brad Robertson - a poet I admire - for reading and advising me during the writing process. I finally thank James Brian Moulder for the drawings which illuminate the collection.

Ivy League

They wrap, they grow, they seek out fresh blood
to fill the veins of their hallways
through recruitment, through prestige,
perhaps, to the lucky, through invitation.

Only ever striving higher, climbing,
sometimes inches at a time,
crawling like a vine, but surely, gradually,
the ivy reaches every goal it sets,
wrapping around all of academia,
its soft reach ever-expanding out,
and only, like any vine, upward.

How funny now to think back
on the origin of the name itself,
on Caswell Adams who, in envy,
referred to those old schools,
covered wall-to-wall in vines
as exactly that: The "Ivy League."

Once meant to imply a staleness,
an oldness, an overgrowth,
yet only to grow, as if by design,
into a beloved nickname, a catchphrase,
a piece of their history like any other.
For what is the nature of a vine
if not to take such a thing for itself?

Van Wickle gates

How majestic the wrought iron gates
that claim this space for Brown,
betwixt brick posts laid by artisans,
wrapped in angles and curves
of blackened metal, old and strong,
always welcoming scholars home.

How triumphant the decorative peak
above the space where they meet,
metalwork flowing like delicate waves,
crashing against the smooth curve,
threateningly precise, intimately perfect,
designed between decadence and grace.

The feeling of walking through them,
the pride, the hubris, the ecstasy
of being wrapped in their opulence,
even for a moment, as you pass by,
guided in like a king to his castle
by such extravagant, purposeful artistry.

To live like this, to work like this,
to study within these fairytale gates,
safe from the worries of the world,
inside an exclusive club of learners.
An entire intently devoted student body
enclosed, like precious pearls.

Blowing in the wind

A girl blows bubbles beneath the breeze,
swaying softly without a care.
Brown campus is just a background,
a canvas against which to strike
all the paints of a young lady's joys.

Entranced for a moment, I pause to watch
as the bubbles bounce and wobble about,
soaring in an airborne stumbling way,
sometimes popping soon, sometimes late,
occasionally merging or tackling siblings.

Much like a human's ambitions, honestly,
though impossible to tell, of course,
if the rainbow colors of dripping soap
best suit any one person's dreams.
Yet here they are. Here they soar.

Some try hard to rise to the clouds.
Some do not make it far at all.
All eventually, with finality, pop,
leaving only a thin, slippery residue
to fall back to the earth below.

Is that the fate of a fresh-formed dream?
To fly as high as it possibly can
only to someday wiggle too much
and burst, unceremoniously ended?
Perhaps it is. Perhaps it isn't.

Far better though to believe not.
A dream that fell back to earth
long after the passing of its master
might still float beautifully,
slick with that rainbow-soap.

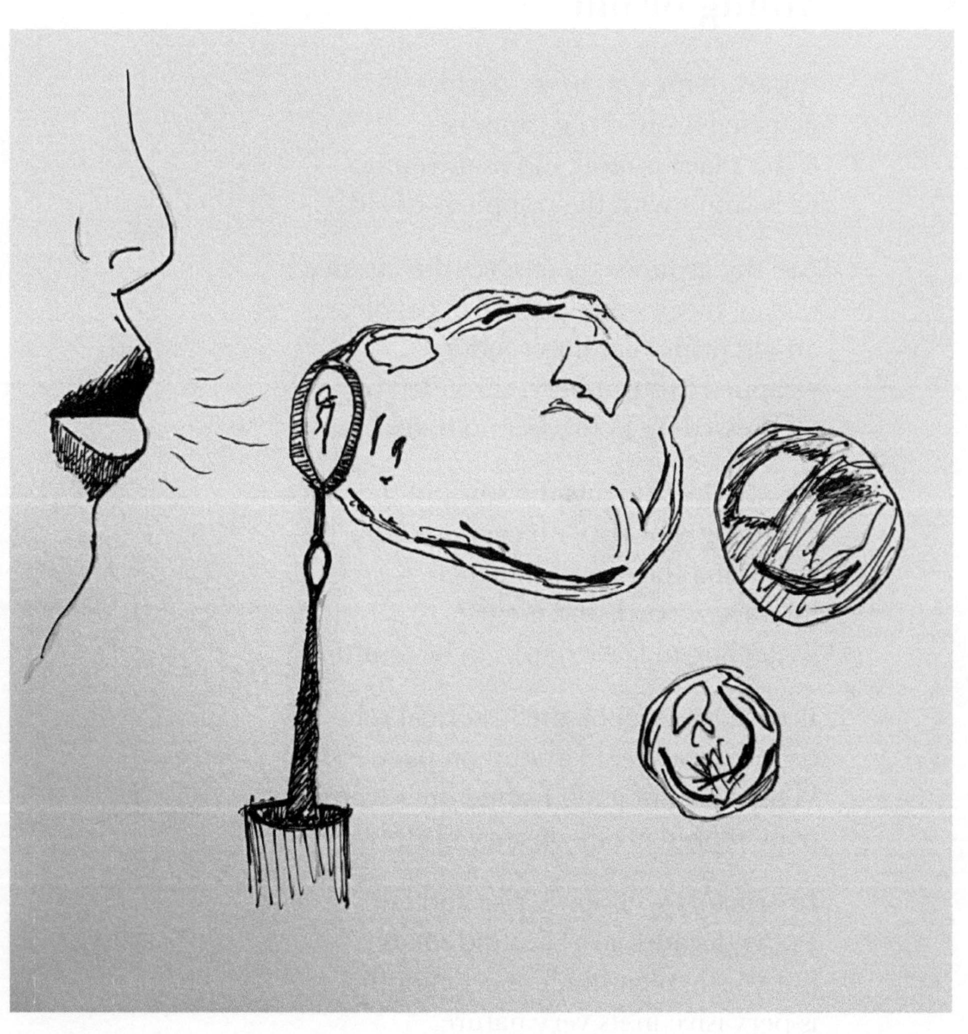

Young or old

A part of me can never decide,
glancing around the campus,
if this place is more old than young,
or is youth with the trappings of old.

Are the grounds themselves the essence,
oozing history and a sense of privilege,
an old pride that never fades,
wrapped in shrubbery, shrouded by trees,
all dressed up in bricks and books?

Or are the students the spirit of the place,
changing quickly with every season,
spreading their own influence
into every crack and crevice,
struggling to leave marks to be found?

Is the library book the historical relic
or the decades old graffiti on page 53?
Which part of it all, I sometimes wonder,
truly represents the history of Brown?

Instructors will slowly rise and fall
as the decades swirl around them
but youth, plentiful innocent youth,
is pervasive in its very nature.
Perhaps timelessness is built on this,
where young and old can coexist.

De Humani Corporis Fabrica

(Andreas Vesalius in the Hay Library)

Our identities are etched across books of flesh
fitted to these frail and mortal forms,
from race to gender to age, all penned out,
whether we accept those words or not.
Yet we tear at it, we scratch at it,
we rip away as much as we can, greedily,
leaving behind such gross and empty patches
that we then fill with law, reason and anatomy.

Take then the man who did nothing, often.
How beautiful and broad he was,
how comfortable wearing his own skin,
his own story as if he knew it to be a gift.
How vapid his expressions, how empty his head,
to just wander aimlessly past shelves,
wanting for nothing and taking nothing.
Imagine, then, how envious I was of that.

Do not blame me, I beg of you,
I, who am so uncomfortable within my book
of flesh to which I have been prescribed
for my envy, my desire, my lust for his life
if I had to carve him up, quietly, gently,
artfully sliding a Stanley knife
between the teres major and latissimus dorsi,
creating new leather, and a brand-new cover.

chimaphilia maculata

College kids coming in skirts and shorts,
covering the campus in giggles and snorts
as I marvel at how little I missed them all
and hope and pray for a short, quick Fall.
This, among seasons, is perhaps the loudest
when the kids are at their proudest,
before the humility of the year can sink in
while I linger at my door, just to drink in
that precious moment before I have to leave
as I wave away Summer's brief reprieve.

I stop to admire a striped wintergreen,
the chimaphilia maculata, ever serene.
One lone bloom happened out of season
as if committed to a smooth, silent treason.
A single white flower droops, bows, and nods
above its evergreen leaves and slender rods.
From its budding 't was doomed to live alone,
serving only to adorn the moment it shone.

Perhaps that's not so bad in a way, you know.
To live for the moments when you best grow.
This grief-stricken bloom that barely stands
may have had no other needs or demands
than to have this moment, removed from peers
so that it might gleam like a newborn's tears
amidst the growing waves of orange and red
that into Autumn's streets have slowly bled.

Autumn's magics

(An Elisabethan Rhapsody)

Lo and behold how the leaves flare up,
flooding the sky with reds, oranges, yellows,
as if to bathe me in a sea of soft fire,
meant for admiring, for crunching underfoot,
for children to dive into headfirst,
swimming in these gentle, crispy flames,
crackling with laughter in their piles
while the adults look on in solemn respect,
feeling the passage of time kiss their foreheads
as unseeable immortals walk the halls
of the groves, the forests, tapping each branch,
leaving only the traces of faery fires behind.

But most of all, behold the green ash tree,
though it is ironically golden today,
steeped in the divine, relentless glimmer
of Queen Titania herself, who kisses it
with such fervor, such entrancing opulence
as if only to make Oberon roll in his sleep,
fearful of losing his queen to an old sapling.
You can almost hear her giggle in its leaves,
dreaming of all the pranks there are to pull,
whispering sweet nothings to the children,
while I stare, nearly breaking into tears,
into those grand gilded cloudlike branches.

BROWN

Ode to a football helmet

This brownish metal cuplike trinket
born to bolster some young buck's head,
this football helmet, by the shrubs,
signaling the passing of warrior heroes,
American men in American sports,
empty, unable to protect in this state.

Wherefrom did you come, helmet?
Are you forgotten or abandoned here?
Oh, to see that youngling return, blushing,
to reclaim one piece of precious gear,
for if they do not, which they may not,
then surely, at length, 't is forgotten.

If so, then it may never again bask
upon the brow of a young warrior,
destined only to someday be swept away.
An emblem of masculinity, of bravado,
bedding on piles of browning leaves,
tragically lost, momentarily found.

Whisper into me the unknown name
of that man-cub you did once protect.
If you only could, with all the vigor
worthy of such a well-worn helm,
perhaps with a spring in my step,
I might then, only then, reunite you.

Hollering voices

Hollering voices that bellow nearby
Interrupt my thinking as I tilt toward the sky
praying, hoping that today will fly by,
I hold my head with a sigh
because the clinking cans, and stamping feet
Mark students approaching and marching to seats
that I might not mind if they did not fill
so that I could longer linger in my cell
undisturbed, unperturbed by their presence
and all the more grateful for their absence.

But no! My day will be a tale to sing about,
not one of a man who festers and pouts.
I will emerge, and even as I'm submerged
in the loud crowd of Fall, converged
around my feeble frame, I will still remain
in control of myself. This is my domain!

I have students to teach atop these hills,
even if it be against their wills,
and I will shout meaning into their brains
until they return to society, slightly more sane
than when they arrived as mere children
who partied too much, not yet beholden
to the laws, the rules, that govern a life.
They don't know much of age or strife,
but I will prepare them for what lies ahead
and give all I have, till I am dead.
For if I am to bloom only once a year,
let it be without dread; let it be without fear.

Surround me with all the noises I hate.
Winter's not yet, but I can wait.
I will abuse the time that Autumn gives
so that December can live.

Brown Bookstore

(et in arcadia ego)

Between the on-trend tones around
I find that silence oft abounds,
a place to hide, my solemn sanctum
where the pages glow
reflecting the luminescent lights
across the chairs I've grown to know.

The wide margins on the pages
act like mental barricades,
cascading walls of whitewashed planes,
upon which fiction lives,
creating worlds for my escape,
wrapped round me, ear to ear
like mid-Winter's fuzzy capes
when the colder months are here.

But it's when the windows frost
and the fade away begins again
that I no longer feel so lost
amidst the icy crystals then,
more ready to soften my grin,
for while my brow may tighten
when the noise around distracts,
it is always the bookstore that protects
the pieces I lack.

Festival of the written harvest

Cornhusking, how funny the word, the usage,
the absurdity that a term belonging to the harvest,
to farmers, to hardy mud-kneed men of the field,
would become literature, as a flood of anthologies
crops up against the walls of bookstores
like so many ears of corn on their stalks.

Anthology, anthology, you share in this, too,
old word born of ancient flower arrangement.
How funny that books, made up of paper,
might return to nature in the magic of words,
in the ridiculous complexity of etymology,
in hidden stories that are never told in the tomes.

"Best of." They all say it, they all claim it.
Each anthology of this year's harvest
sits on the shelf with those words printed,
as if to whisper something pretentious.
You are all from a handful of publishers.
So "best of" what, then? Liars. Charlatans.

Give me instead a good *divan*, if you would.
Mercilessly husk away the dead leaves
of mediocre poetry, of words I will not miss,
leaving me only the best, the finest crops
and let me grow fat on corn and flowers
harvested from only the finest fields.

Ann's apple pies

Lovely landlady Ann, who I know
to be a Polish lass of humble stock,
a devout Catholic, true to her faith,
but a bit too young to be a widow.

Embodies New England well
in her apple pies, so flavorful,
so full of authenticity, sincerity,
with just the perfect sweetness.

Filling that softens and shrinks
within a hard, crisp brown crust,
hard then soft like people.
So very, very much like us.

Summer to Fall to Winter flows
as she bakes to her heart's desire.
Low-medium heat in a Dutch oven
that smells, faintly, of fruit.

I spy lemon juice and cinnamon
sprinkled with care throughout,
sweetening it all with sugar,
as she smiles a sweet, sad smile.

I wonder what does the widow think
as she bakes the pie her lover praised?
Each scent is a whiff of cultures colliding,
each bite a bittersweet memory to taste.

Pumpkin Carving

(For Alexander Shamana)

The plump pumpkins amidst stumps and roots
nestled betwixt the chrysanthemums of the garden
seem to call out, crying for a carving.

Eager to remember the taste of Fall,
-the sickening sweetness -
I reach for one twice the size of a human head
thinking already of who to carve, or what.

It could be a president of the modern era, with a mocking grin
or perhaps a historical figure, vigorously reimagined
by the swipes of a sharpened knife.

It could be a serial killer, a wrestler with a cowlick,
a slasher from the flicks apropos for the season,
too fearful for the kiddies of the neighborhood.

Infinite options circle my head. I think, for a moment,
that perhaps it could be me. A self-portrait in pumpkin,
that most seasonal of mediums.

But alas I am not as easy to carve as I once was,
for each wrinkle beside my eyes must be accounted for,
painstakingly recreated from scratch.

Far better, in a sense, to carve someone young, beautiful
for the lack of effort it would take, the lack of lines to make
in order to evoke an accurate image.

But then, perhaps it's the difficulty of the wrinkles
and the challenge of capturing the wear and tear of life itself
that makes the carving all the better.

I laugh because I know I'm overthinking something as simple,
as supple, and as silly as a plump, grinning, little pumpkin.
A pumpkin carving need not be perfect.
It exists because it exists, being only to be.

Autumn, betrayer

Ah, but I do remember when I loved
the Fall with all its promises intact.
It's common, of course, for youth
to flush red with the leaves, thinking
of the shorts and skirts coming back
while the holidays come blazing through
bringing us home to where we long
and back into each other's arms amidst
the pumpkins and the turkey dinners.

But now. Those same blood-red leaves
chill me to my deepest bones,
more frigid, less forgiving than ice –
I despise the racket, the unbearable
pacing of any season that tears me out
of the void-blessed absences of Winter.
Where is my snow now? Its crystal splendor
whispered such sweet promises before,
only to prove deceitful, like its cousin,
just as Autumn once betrayed me
now too does Winter turn her back,
digging her cold shoulder into my spine.

I forgive you, sweet chilling winds.
I forgive you, Jack Frost, if and only if
you fly home to me at once, bringing
your peace, your quiet, my sanctum
back to me, so that my weary head
may rest upon my bed again, please.
Give back to me what I once had
before I ever had Meniere's disease.

The wrestler's injury

He who loves to pin down his foes,
wrapped scarcely in a singlet,
forcibly asserting competitive dominance
with passion befitting the Trojan War.

Once noble wrestler, sleek and powerful,
how odd to hear how you now babble.
A minor concussion, too minor to notice,
but enough to snap a synapse or two
out of whatever place was meant for them
and now, too late, we see the damage.

Still, a nearly ordinary daily life.
Ice cream cones on Coney Island.
Making sweet but distant love
to a cheap Italian movie star.

Followed by an oddball, a weirdo,
or so the half-addled boy says.
A weirdo who makes soap out of people
all gathered by the warm old fire
between helter skelters and the Spookhouse.

Hang in there, man, long as you can.
Hold onto each memory within,
each victory on the wrestling mat,
each love cradled in your mind.
Keep your head safe and kind.

The dinner bell

He spent all morning prattling on
about flowers and Winter again
while I watched the clock tick tock
past eight, past nine, past ten.
Y'all might've had the patience
to listen to his caterwauling
about how much he misses snow
But I am just here bawling
because my copious dinner
Is gonna get colder while I get slimmer
waiting for Teach to shut his trap.
It's not that I don't give a crap,
but a hungry stomach hurts me so
Much, his fixation on ice and snow
can shove it for a while, alright?
I just want some turkey tonight.

Yeah, I get that it's commercialized.
It was supposed to be about gratitude,
and we got the meaning a little twisted,
but can all the high-ground platitudes
and the lectures wait, just a minute?
I am grateful, but also, I just want the food.
It's not that I'm not listening, alright?
And I really, truly don't mean to be rude.

The snow's great, cool, okay, yes
but could you control yourself
because I'm straining my ears
to hear that sweet silver bell
that means I can run on out
to the tables and help myself
to the supper I'm longing for.

You love the snow and that's great
but I don't. I'm Southern-raised
so just give me some fried fowl
or maybe some short ribs, braised,
but either way keep that crippling frost
in your dreams where it belongs
and try to be grateful for the warmth
that you'll miss when it's gone.

Old Thayer Street

For Sérgio

Give me a place to drink and to eat
nestled somewhere on old Thayer Street,
between the shops and the cinema,
I desire only one moment of peace
and hope to find it waiting for me
at a wooden table beside Thayer Street.

Bring me a beverage, a pastry please,
to celebrate one more slow-moving day
and let me rest my weary feet
here beside bustling, hustling, old Thayer Street.

There truly has never been more bliss
than stretching your legs upon old roads,
amidst calm and confident stores
that have long since proven their worth
to both students and travelers alike.
So if you would have my day be complete,
then buy me a dinner on good old Thayer Street.

Et in Ithaca ego

Visiting Cornell with Daan.

I celebrate swollen holes in my soul,
relaxed on the altar of Sage Chapel.
I lay three precious gifts down carefully,
- Chaney, Goodman, and Schwerner -
Victims of an ancient recurring crime.
Brought low from the palaces on the slope
and raise my glass of maple syrup high.

How better, I think in jest, to honor
brutal loss than with sickening sweetness,
thick on my lips like blood in broad daylight.

Staring at denominational voids.
Telemachus hides here in a pewter,
that brat who is supposed to be my son.
Who'd best Paris for Achilles' tendon?
He lost his muse listing to Mrs. Cornell,
making his hands dirty on the cogwheels.
Fatty oils swell under clawed, filthy nails.

Wash them in the old Delaware waters.
Let some history soak those crevasses
while modernity laughs, often in vain.

One hand on my heart. That old anthem plays.
Days with Circe and Calliope fade,
the tricuspid valve contracting deep, low.
Lub-dub, lub-dub, lub- dub, lub-dub… dub-lub?
Mr. Morse sends secret messages in blank verse:
You are the foretold one-eyed wonderer,
You are the designated survivor.

Grieving

The mud that clumps up well beneath my windowsill
leads me to linger as a moment of strained silence
drives through, before the pounding rain above
resounds through the rafters, bringing me back.

How ugly Fall seems, upon these repugnant puddles
Buried in rotting orange and brown leaves, infested
with insects of each shape and size that feast
on the leftovers, the dead dregs of vegetation.

Halloween came and went, its drunken parties
now retreating back into that mysterious haze
from which holidays seem to come and go
as the decorations languish in clearance aisles.

Still, the shadow of its presence is felt here
amidst the disgusting, desecrated Jack-o-lanterns
that deteriorate on nearby doorsteps, their owners
too slobby to remove them, or too sentimental.

What was once a well-lit grin is now true horror
as flies buzz in and out of a sloppy wet mass
that looks more pulp than plant, its hollow eyes
drooping into an expression of regret… grieving.

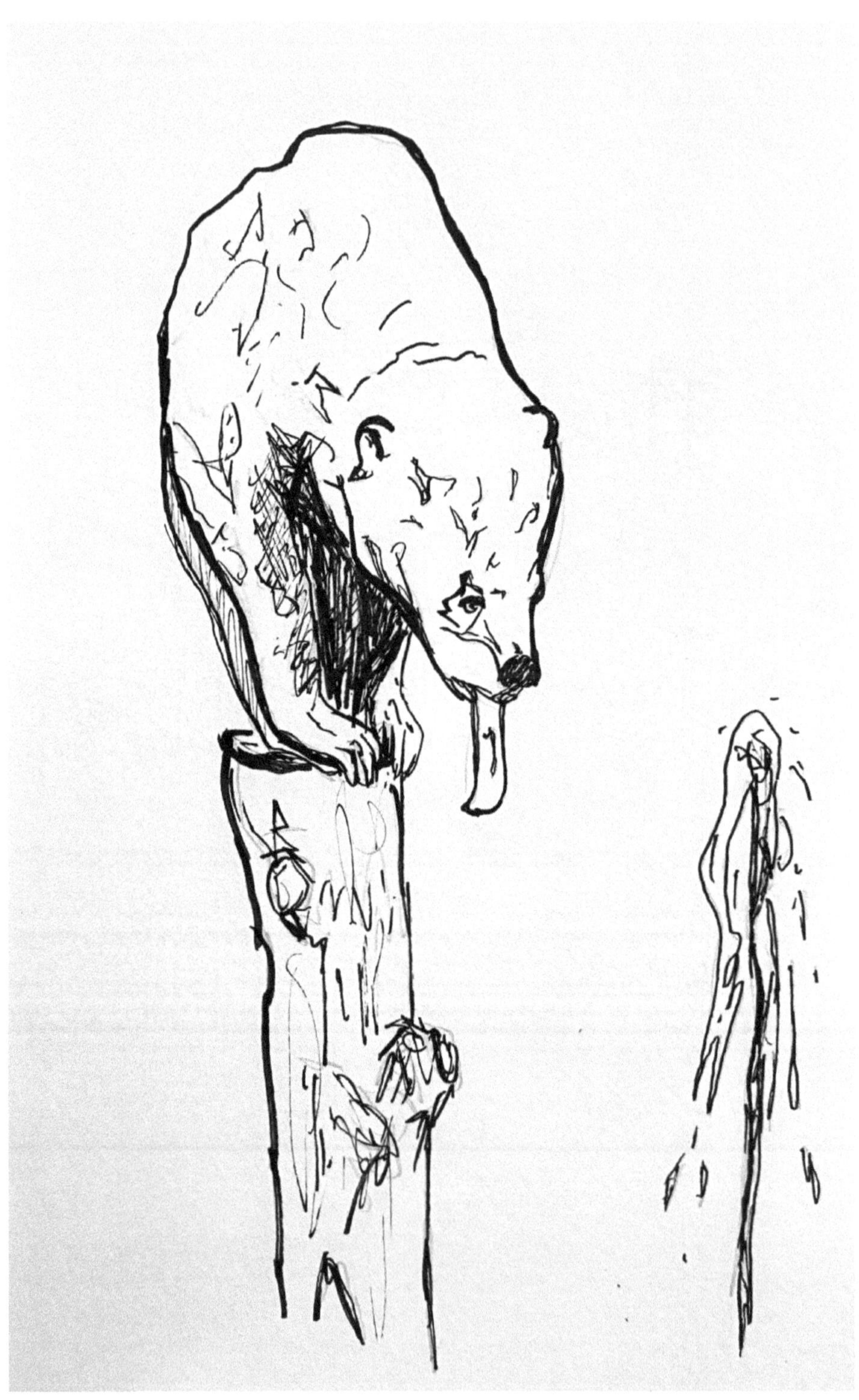

Of Little Bear Fountain

Odd little bear upon your perch,
forged of bronze to rest here.
How refreshing the water must be
where this silly bear does drink.

Do you remember Theodore F. Green,
who gifted you to this quiet place?
Or do you stare on in complacency,
content to fill space amidst the foliage?
What might you have witnessed,
little bear, in seven decades here?
Would that you could whisper
all seventy plus years of gossip.

How funny, how quirky, to just be a bear,
built of bronze, by the Faculty Club.
To exist solely to decorate a space,
yet seem so home. It's quietly great.

What a welcome sight you are, oh bear,
who guards a little water beneath you,
though no others seek to be you.
For you are a humble statue here,
surrounded by great and famous faces
from every era of human history.
How fitting then, to just be a bear,
striking your own pose so happily.

The straight-backed horseman

For Zac

Marcus Aurelius, how I envy you so
up on your horse upon the pedestal
without any sense that you could sway,
as unwavering today as any other.

You do not wear stirrups on your feet
but the straight line of your still back
seems to lack uncertainty, as you point
proudly off toward a sight I cannot see.

While here am I, wobbly and weak
as the stirrups and anvils in my ear
fail me, not prevailing as they should
even though I stand on my own two feet.

You upon your horse, Marcus Aurelius,
may have been wise to not wear stirrups.
Would I, perhaps, stand half as proud
if I could see what you point toward?

Greyhound busdriver

Loyal greyhound, coming and going,
full of students who live nearby,
a few teachers, clutching their things,
tightly trying not to be noticed.

An elderly couple sits at the front,
just in front of the children who curse,
yet to no one does this seem strange,
this odd arrangement of unlikely souls.

A man wearing a reflective vest
reads a newspaper, tips his hardhat down
to block the encroaching rays
of a swiftly setting distant sun.

I think, for a moment, how strange it is
that only I am bothered by this,
the crowds unseparated, unsorted,
each living their lives even in transit.

The driver barely seems bothered.
Not by the seated, nor the luggage,
only commenting on anyone's clutter
if it blocks the aisle for the others.

What an odd career it must be
to sit silently at the front of it all,
this distinctly different mismatched throng
of wonderful characters, so alive and free.

Visiting Harvard Campus

I remember wondering about John Harvard's face.
I was, at the time, strangely fixated on his hat.
What did the legend himself wear while alive?
Surely an obscenely high, costly hat
worthy of his status, flauntingly daunting
in its magnificence, stitched with more hides
than a mere mortal could afford way back when.

Surely I would see a painting portraying him
somewhere, softly speaking without moving,
passing a legacy forward from his frame,
so imagine my disdain when I learned
they'd long since burned and my yearning
to know a historic portraiture would be sated
instead, oddly, by a cold, unfeeling statue.
I was not reeling for long, for the strong
visage instantly seared itself into my vision.

And he did seem alive, in the moment,
as I gently wiped the snow from his feet,
feeling nearly defeated beneath
the imposing figure that presided there,
rising so much higher than me, alive,
even so very long after his death.

To think that a hatless man in a chair
could radiate eminence so intimately,
looking as if his lips might loosen
to tell me stories of the distant past,
of Puritans, parchment, and permanence,
tales built even to outlast time itself.

As many do, I caressed the feet of the statue,
hoping for good luck, admiring the shine
of the bronze where it'd been rubbed raw,
while I gently, meticulously removed
piles of snow from around his shoes
as if concerned that he might be cold.

The Declaration of Dependence

Forgive me when my feet stray,
for I do not mean to block you.
I'm often told to adjust my step
but adjust it how, I wonder?
There is no "straight ahead" for me
so I'm left to blindly ponder.

You all walk as the wise men did,
guided one way by a sacred star.
But mine refuses to shine for me
so my feet slip, skate and stray.
It's not that I mean to run into you
but I just can't seem to find my way.

My brain forms crooked constellations
and tells me to seek out the center.
I can only lunge forward toward them,
my false stars that line the ground.
I don't mean to be a bother, friend,
but my footsteps have been bound.

It's an unfair lesson in humility
as I'm forced to ask the way again.
But I will admit my path is missing
if it means you'll guide me then.
Please tell me where the star is
so I can stride like way back when
I walked as straight a path as you
with no dishonest stars to blind me
back when forward seemed so true
and my thoughts did not bind me.

Endless wonderland.

How wonderful it would be for the plastic spiderwebs
on the porches to be buried beneath the crystal threads
of freshly fallen snow as it cradles the landscape,
though I know it will be a while yet. I wait.

Ever so patient, for what good is a half-woven web?
If it takes weeks or years to fall, I will be here
to admire the works of art that descend from the sky
as they invisibly whisper out words of encouragement.

Weave your webs well, Old Man Winter, please
so that they never fade again once they fall to earth.
Weave for me a tapestry of never-melting snow
so that next Halloween be celebrated on ice.

Lend me an endless wonderland of soft, silent silk
so that I might cover the rotting pumpkins with it,
cleansed, never to be seen again, overtaken by slush
and tranquility. I tire of their languid faces.

I know that this wish is not to be, that the snow
will be only temporary, but bring it now
so that I might at least dream, while I pretend
it will never cease. Please, set Winter free.

The restless snow

for William

The settling silvers of a snowglobe
catch my eye, freezing me for a moment,
my feet fettered to the spot, tethered
by the rigid ropes of a ragged mind.

I remember my doctor's descriptions
of the messiness of Meniere's disease.
Tiny crystals rattle about my head,
like snow that will never settle.

Circling, circling, swirling, swirling,
serving only to usurp my sanity
as I stumble, tumble, stand my ground,
still unwilling to give in to it now.

No wonder then that I love snow,
in which peace triumphs over all
as the pure crystals romantically rest,
each flake falling keenly into place.

If only my ears could snow like that
instead of like an aimless blizzard.
If only everything would stand still,
like in the dead of Winter it naturally will.

Spinning of the seasons

The snow that covered the landscape lightens,
bringing my breath to a halt
because I know, instantly, instinctively
that my beloved Winter will wither soon.

Already the flowers begin to bud once more
and the grass seems greener than before
and while I should, perhaps, be glad
I only dread the days ahead, as my warm bed
seems to fade into memory, the silence
I'd come to love so much gives way now
gradually, seamlessly, to the idle yelps
of the young and the bustle of busywork.

I would sell my soul for the sweet silent snow
but instead I fight off a dizzy spell
knowing well that the damnable tides of Spring
are well and truly upon me, oppressing me.

Take not my irritation for a child's irreverence;
Please do not assume or presume that I,
in my years, have been always so weary.
I too once looked forward to this.

But now the brightness burns me bald with worry
as I think on all the work ahead, the fires of Hell
tickling my toes while the flowers arrogantly bloom
where once there was peaceful quiet beauty.

Thawning

The chilled and cheery aesthetic of a raging blizzard
suits the chaos of my mind, the spinning, the spinning,
far more than some insipid lukewarm breeze ever could
but I do not blame Spring, I suppose, for this.

My preferences are my own, to be sure.
I am not such a prideful prude as to insist
that I am not in small ways sick, but still
am I not entitled to wish? Farewell, Winter.

I barely knew your blissful blow,
seeing only now the negligence I meted out
as the leaves pop out of their branches,
blotting out the silent whiteness that grew on me.

Already I hear it. The shriek of rubber on the streets
as the depleted masses flock to bother me again.
The minute they kick out from their unkempt beds
the unwashed many must multiply and emaciate
every facet of the hard-earned peace I yearned for
because of course they must, they must so unjustly
spit upon the fabric of solitude, the sinless white snows
melting all the faster beneath the breath of cars.

But yes, all hail Spring in his infinite wisdom
so beloved by all for his poetic place in love itself
even as his excessive exuberance drives
his gnawing nails back into my aching head.

There is meaning

I sigh. There is some meaning in this
momentary time in my life when leaves fade
from a lively green to a crackling, bloody red.
Yet now I dodge the crisp little leaves
like landmines littered about the lawns
for even their crunch would not be so silent
as it once was, back when I was amused
by the strange fragility of life as it snapped
beneath my carefree feet, never knowing
that I would (someday soon) know this frailty.

Come back into my waiting arms, Winter,
my void-blessed lady of the ice and snow
who whispers into my ears such promises
of a forever silence, though I still know
that it cannot be so, that you will leave me,
for you are, after all, an unfaithful lady.
To which distant shore have you gone,
while I wilt in the indecency of your absence?

To which distant shore must I go,
to glow once more, like blood on your snow,
my moments of madness seeming charming
against your soft, forgiving backdrop?
I gladly give myself unto you, my Winter,
if you would only promise me a reprieve,
a momentary peace, a blessing with which
to stave off the disease, the lawless screaming
of the world as it circles inside my brain.

So yes, I do accept the unjust blasphemy
of despising a season that I can never reclaim
if I'll sooner have Winter in my arms again
as compensation for the shortening of this life
that I would gladly live less of, but alone with her.

Printed by Libri Plureos GmbH in Hamburg,
Germany